How to Paint Sunlight

LAWRENCE FERLINGHETTI

How to Paint Sunlight

LYRIC POEMS & OTHERS

(1997–2000)

A NEW DIRECTIONS BOOK

Book design by Sylvia Frezzolini Severance
Manufactured in the United States of America
New Directions Books are printed on acid-free paper.
First published clothbound by New Directions in 2001
Published simultaneously in Canada by Penguin Books, Canada Limited

Library of Congress Cataloging-in-Publication Data
Ferlinghetti, Lawrence.
How to paint sunlight : lyric poems & others (1997-2000)/
Lawrence Ferlinghetti.
p. cm.
Includes indexes.
ISBN 0-8112-1463-X (acid-free paper)
I. Title.
PS3511.E557 H6   2001
811'.54—dc21   00-067860

New Directions Books are published for James Laughlin
by New Directions Publishing Corporation
80 Eighth Avenue, New York 10011

Contents

FOR ALBERTINE

A WORD

"All I wanted to do was paint sunlight on the side of a house," said Edward Hopper (or words to that effect), and there have been legions of poets and filmmakers obsessed with light. I would side with the irrational visionary romantic who says light came first, and darkness but a fleeting shadow to be swept away with more light. ("More light!" cried the great novelist, dying.) Poets and painters are the natural bearers of it, and all I ever wanted to do was paint light on the walls of life. These poems are another attempt to do it.

—Lawrence Ferlinghetti

How to Paint Sunlight

INSTRUCTIONS TO PAINTERS & POETS

I asked a hundred painters and a hundred poets
how to paint sunlight
on the face of life
Their answers were ambiguous and ingenuous
as if they were all guarding trade secrets
Whereas it seems to me
all you have to do
is conceive of the whole world
and all humanity
as a kind of art work
a site-specific art work
an art project of the god of light
the whole earth and all that's in it
to be painted with light

And the first thing you have to do
is paint out postmodern painting
And the next thing is to paint yourself
in your true colors
in primary colors
as you see them
(without whitewash)
paint yourself as you see yourself
without make-up
without masks
Then paint your favorite people and animals
with your brush loaded with light

And be sure you get the perspective right
and don't fake it
because one false line leads to another

And then paint the high hills
when the sun first strikes them
on an autumn morning
With your palette knife
lay it on
the cadmium yellow leaves
the ochre leaves
the vermillion leaves
of a New England autumn
And paint the ghost light of summer nights
and the light of the midnight sun
which is moon light
And don't paint out the shadows made by light

for without chiaroscuro you'll have shallow pictures
So paint all the dark corners too
everywhere in the world
all the hidden places and minds and hearts
which light never reaches
all the caves of ignorance and fear
the pits of despair
the sloughs of despond
and write plain upon them
"Abandon all despair, ye who enter here"

And don't forget to paint
all those who lived their lives

as bearers of light
Paint their eyes
and the eyes of every animal
and the eyes of beautiful women
known best for the perfection of their breasts
and the eyes of men and women
known only for the light of their minds
Paint the light of their eyes
the light of sunlit laughter
the song of eyes
the song of birds in flight

And remember that the light is within
if it is anywhere
and you must paint from the inside
Start with purity
with pure white
the pure white of gesso
the pure white of cadmium white
the pure white of flake white
the pure virgin canvas
the pure life we all begin with

Turner painted sunlight
with egg tempera
(which proved unstable)
and Van Gogh did it with madness
and the blood of his ear
(also unstable)
and the Impressionists did it
by never using black

and the Abstract Expressionists did it
with white house paint
But you can do it with the pure pigment
(if you can figure out the formula)
of your own true light
But before you strike the first blow
on the virgin canvas
remember its fragility
life's extreme fragility
and remember its innocence
its original innocence
before you strike the first blow

Or perhaps never strike it
And let the light come through
the inner light of the canvas
the inner light of the models posed
in the life study
the inner light of everyone
Let it all come through
like a pentimento
the light that's been painted over
the life that's been painted over
so many times
Let it all surge to the surface
the painted-over image
of primal life on earth

And when you've finished your painting
stand back astonished

stand back and observe
the life on earth that you've created
the lighted life on earth
that you've created
a new brave world

THE CHANGING LIGHT

The changing light at San Francisco
        is none of your East Coast light
           none of your
                pearly light of Paris
The light of San Francisco
        is a sea light
           an island light
And the light of fog
        blanketing the hills
      drifting in at night
        through the Golden Gate
           to lie on the city at dawn
And then the halcyon late mornings
      after the fog burns off
      and the sun paints white houses
          with the sea light of Greece
     with sharp clean shadows
       making the town look like
         it had just been painted
But the wind comes up at four o'clock
              sweeping the hills
And then the veil of light of early evening
And then another scrim
      when the new night fog
           floats in
And in that vale of light
      the city drifts
         anchorless upon the ocean

YACHTS IN SUN

The yachts the white yachts
    with their white sails in sunlight
        catching the wind and
                heeling over
All together racing now
           for the white buoy
     to tack about
       to come about beyond it
And then come running in
    before the spanking wind
       white spinnakers billowing
          off Fort Mason San Francisco
Where once drowned down
     an Alcatraz con escaping
       whose bones today are sand
              fifty fathoms down
      still imprisoned now
             in the glass of the sea
As the so skillful yachts
      freely pass over

WHITE DREAMS

A dream of white a dream of light
                              a white-out of darkness
        a dream of a white stallion
                              in a dark landscape
            of a naked woman
                              riding it
        a dream of a girl-woman
                  in a long white dress
                        and a picture hat
                              crossing Gatsby's lawn
    and a dream
        of a white horse
              running in an open field
                        her white mane streaming
                        across the autumn landscape
            that some painter has painted
                              with cadmium ochre light
    and a dream of bales of hay in a barn
                        they too painted light ochre
                        where a white mare feeds
                              on ochre grain
    and a dream of early morning again
            when the white light reminds us
                              we are all immortal
        all of us creatures in a field
                        while eternal time trembles
                              in first light

But what of Van Gogh's sun
              as it howling turns round
                            in the twisted firmament
And what of that terrible sun
              and its terrible light
                            shining through Dante's night
And what is that light that never was
                            on land and sea?
What is light What is air What is life so passing fair?
Let some angel answer
                    in a skidrow bar room

BIG SUR LIGHT

1.
What is that sound that fills the air
distantly—
Is that a singing still
a far singing
under the hill
a descant
a threnody
arising
echoing away—
the happiness of animals on earth
forefeet pawing or prancing
or lying still in thickets
And couples dancing
to flute and small drum
the happiness of animals on earth—
or their unhappiness—
their loneliness perhaps
(for are the cries of birds
cries of ecstasy
or cries of despair?)
Ah but the earth is still
so passing fair
in the heart of all our days

2.

The trees in their eternal silence
  follow the dawn
              out of the night
And all is not lost
  when a tree can still
        in first light
      spread its autumn branches
          and let go its ochre leaves
                    in pure delight

3.

How lovely the earth
and all the creatures in it
Shining in eternity
in dearth and death of night
as the sun
    the sun
        shakes out its shining hair
                    of streaming light

4.

The birds slept in this morning
Not a word out of them
until sun up
Usually they're out there
just before light
tuning up

chirring away to themselves
about the nature of light
for which they're always yearning
or about the earth
and why it never stops
turning—
Big questions
for birds to settle
and tell us
in single syllables
before breakfast

5.
Thrushes in the underbrush

Shy birds
never let themselves be seen
Modesty
in their little birdcalls

And always the same notes
(and the same message?)
over and over:
Hello again! hello again! hello?

6.
Clouds sailing over—
Ah there's Magritte's lips
faded out in the rosy dawn!

st month—
ny window

seemed endless
but went on
like the moon
sailing through its dark seas
a lighted ship at sea
Once in a while a plane winged by
soundless
flashing its human signal
in the night of the sky
And the moon sailed on
listing a bit to starboard
looking almost as if
it might capsize
overloaded as it always was
with the reflected
imagined love
of the world
And then at the final end of night

the sea turned white
as the too-full moon
still beat seaward
through its white night
too loaded to land anywhere
with its precious
perishable cargo

8.
   The moon
 after much reflection says
   Sun is God

    *

 The sky full of leaves & pollen
   in the high wind
    sows trees!

    *

  The tree believes
  its panoply of leaves
  will save it from acid rain
   (Think again)

*

Will the rains ever end?
Basho claps together
His muddy clogs

*

Will the world ever end?
Dawn and the sun
runs its fingers
over the land

*

Phallus in vulva
And a divine spasm
Shakes the universe

DICTIONARIES OF LIGHT

The sun the sun
        comes round the corner
           like a shining knight of old
                galloping over the landscape
                    on the horses of morning
And shaking his lance over us
        in trance of night
           awakens us to speak or sing
                to banish death and darkness
And each steed a word
        each verb a stallion
           reared up against all ignorance
Untamed rampant radicals
           in dictionaries of light

Surreal Migrations

portami il girasole impazzito di luce

—Eugenio Montale

I.

My mind is racing
          in the middle of the night
My mind races
          through the darkness
                              around the world
          through the darkness
                    of the world
Toward a tunnel of light

It races through
          the night of Prague
          through Staromak Square
                    with its Jan Hus sculpture
                              reading Love Each Other
                                        And The Truth Will Triumph
It races on
          through the night streets
     Across the Charles Bridge
                    across the river
                              at the heart of Prague
Across the rivers of the world
          Across the Rhine
               Across the Rhone
                    Across the Seine
                         Across the Thames
                                   Across Anna Livia's Liffey

Across Atlantic
    Across Manhattan
        Across great Hudson
                into the heart of America
My heart is racing now
      Across America
          Across Ole Man River
              rolling along

Where is the light?

My heart is racing now
          Across terrific Pacific
    Across the River of Yellow Light
              of Sun Yat Sen
        Across Gandhi's Ganges
              Across Euphrates
      Across the Nile
          Across the Hellespont
     Across Tiber
       Across Arno
         Across Dante's River Styx
             through the medieval darkness
     Into the heart of the tunnel of light
My heart and mind
          are racing now
       together
          on the same beat
              to the same music
It's not the music of *Carmina Burana*

It's the music of Don Giovanni
It's Mozart's Horn Concerto
It's the Yellow Submarine
                    Yellow Submarine
                              Yellow Submarine
There is a sign in the light
                    at the end of the tunnel
I am trying to read it

We are all
            trying to read it

Dark figures dance in it
                    in the half-darkness
Light figures dance in it
                    in the half-light

II.

Rain is falling on a mirror made of sunshine
Absinthe lover full of absence
your eyes elsewhere
      your hyacinth hair
            your naiad air
   your fine nude legs in sun
In olde Europa
Proust and his madeleine
Apollinaire's migraine
Afternoons on the Grande Jatte
The arrogance of André Breton
Little Addie the Housepainter
with the toothbrush moustache
Is Paris burning?
The Valkyries were singing
unter den linden
Lilli Marlene Lilli Marlene
Underneath the lamplight
by the village green
I must arise and go now
We'll find a place away
morning sun with leaves
full upon you
dappled darling
the very idea of love
Heart shot through with holes
a rain of crystal
a loud silence
a far-off singing

Some heard the silence of the sea
Some drank Vichy
Some were shot running
Some were shot against a wall
Some burned singing
Sun eternal firework
Sun the only god remaining
The moon a crystal mirror
                              eternal deceiver
Is love still burning
     Do lovers alone wear sunlight?
Dica darling
               tell me tell me
Love lie with me
                  beyond the sea
The quays black with voyagers
A crowd flows over London Bridge
Hurry up please
Lady Liberty with flaming torch
stands upon her little island
having dropped her French accent
Don't give me your homeless
Jetliners land
without folding their wings
In a dense fog the foghorns
still are sounding
At Ambrose Light the great ships
still grope through it
Dica darling
A crowd flows over Brooklyn Bridge
Hey taxi!

III.

'Westward the star of empire'
        And the territorial imperative
   still the anima
            in the autumn of civilization
Brave figures gesturing
               on the far horizon
Prairie schooners into Pullmans
      into Land Rovers
           four-by-fours
                earth movers
Mobile homes following
           close upon them
    filled with norte americanos
                always on vacation
       checkbooks at the ready

Clear the land! We're comin' through!
   on skyways lined with shopping malls
    and super service stations
      with thirdworld attendants
         speaking the language of the conquered
While we
      speaking the language of empire
        the Latin of our age
    bowl through
      hightailing it over the horizon
         now illuminated night & day

Toward the final mega nirvana
                corporate camelot
                        cyber city of light
To be set up anywhere in the world
           replete with plastic plaster replicas
                    of the wonders of the world
    Venus de Milos on the half shell
        Statues of Liberty at Las Vegas
             Rodin's Thinkers thinking Nothing
          Boulevards paved with Elgin Marbles
                Cultures subcultures and countercultures
                  consumed and reduced
              to one cheap chip
                on the erect silicon penis
                    of one forty-year-old e-trader
                        from the World Bank
While overhead
    visible from everywhere
        huge illuminated billboards
            pulse in the night

And swept with con
        the millions salivate
            under the signs

IV.

Surreal migration of words
somewhere between speech and song
a kind of descant rising
from word to melody
voice of the fourth person singular
voice of the poet rising
to some ecstasis

beat of wings on a counterpane
wind in the live oaks

or on a western morning
in fair weather
autumn hills in full sun
ochre against the blue
earth and sky together
breathing

Surreal migrations of words
from silence to deep song

quivering of arrows or leaves
upon the wind

Phoenician alphabets
about to sing

flights of seabirds
taking wing

bearing us
seaborn
over the horizon

And the air is filled with our cries

New York, New York

let me lightdrench the saddest of men

—Gregory Corso

THE LIGHT OF BIRDS

I early learned to love birds
the light of birds the kingdom of birds
in the high treetops
stricken with light
living their separate
weightless lives
Light years they lived
apart from us
flashing in sunlight
high above Bronx River Parkway
or high on Hudson's Palisades
they flew about
light as leaves
(and they were as leaves
except in the fall
when they did not fall)
calling to each other
over and over
in the upper air
or lost in the sky
as they soared up there
way up behind the reservoir
where we came as kids
chattering like birds
on a Sunday at sundown
and played in the falling light
and heard for the first time
the distant muffled caws
of our own night

JOURNAL NOTES TURNING INTO A POEM

The birth certificate says 106 Saratoga Avenue Yonkers. . . .
I take the A train to 168th Street, transfer to #1 and continue
on the Elevated to Van Cortland Park, then catch a bus north
to South Yonkers. It's only a mile or more along the west
edge of the park to Carroll Avenue. I get off here on the vague
advice of the old black busdriver who waves in the direction
he thinks Saratoga Avenue might be. . . .

And so uphill half a mile on foot
past blocks of dark brick apartment houses
their better days behind them
And there's the end of Saratoga Avenue
with a mom-and-pop grocery—
An old white man comes out
carrying a quart in a paper sack—
He looks through me
as if I were part of the street
and had been there forever
(Perhaps I have) . . .

I have no memory of the house
                                    or its location
It is as if I am looking for
                                someone else's birthplace
(Perhaps I am)
A slight rain
                starting to fall in the falling light

I pick up my pace
                    hurrying along
Maybe three short blocks
                    to *106*
        where in a small back bedroom
            my brother said he heard my first cry
                            seventy-seven years ago
                    (It echoes now
                            as if I myself had heard it)
The little house
            almost to the crest of the low hill
                a gabled wood-frame house
                    two stories with an attic
                            detached from close-by houses
            A yard with old cars on one side
        And a steep drop in back to a gully
            with a few tall trees
                old barren oaks and elms—
                            bare ruined choirs!
The house itself run down now
Ugly asbestos siding over the old wood
And a small screened-in front porch
Inside the flimsy screen door
    there's a once-handsome oak front door
            with worn brass doorknob and bevelled glass
                upon which goldleaf numerals still show *106*
                (with half the *1* missing)

Three doorbells (three apartments now?)
I ring them all

with no answer
No one in sight anywhere inside
No sign of life or light in nearby houses
A kind of country slum
but still a quiet family neighborhood
Across the little street
            some Latinos with boom-box turned down
                        are hanging out
I walk around back
            by the old cars and the bare trees
                        and look up at the silent house
                                    looking for that small back bedroom
Kikiriki goes a bird just once
                                    like an echo of light
I have been here before?
An incredible
            inexplicable
                        feeling of happiness
                                    floods up from nowhere
The rain increases
It's really coming down now . . .
Let it come down!

Thus be recorded my birthplace
            and how I came upon it
                for the second time
                        maybe three hundred yards north
                            of the northwest corner
                                        of Van Cortlandt Park
                        in a grey rain
                                    seventy-seven years later

It must have been all country back then

The kids must have played ball
                in this green park with its worn diamond
                        and its ancient rusted screen
                            behind the batter's box
I can hear the bat hit the ball
                            (perhaps pitched by Pop)
And my brother running for first base
                                ended up in Baltimore
                                forty years later
And I here
            his interrogator
                        still listening for the sound
        of my vanished family
                            echoing there

Shouts and laughter
                tears and whispers
                            fill the air

MANHATTAN MAMA

Those stone canyons again
Alone as usual
in the heartless canyons
the straight endless streets
hard arteries
in the heart of the beast
The homeless huddled
outside the stone churches

In the Public Library
on West 53d Street
a guard goes around
waking up the street people
or what used to be called bums
sitting asleep with books spread out
in front of them
In the men's room so-called
the graffitti says
       Cathlic church
              had Peter Sellers
                    mudered
Across the street
the Museum of Modern Art
is about to open
The hanging banners say
MOMA
You're not supposed to

pronounce it Mama
though a Jewish Mom
may be running the place
You don't get in free
and there's no chicken soup
and this ain't no
Frank O'Hara lunch poem
The guards act
like they don't like me
though I'm part Jewish
What do they know
Why are poets & painters so paranoid
It shows in their work
All that hostility
Let's throw out all that
leisure-class postmodern artwork
and let the real artists of life
get in there
the ones across the street
sleeping on their books
until they get rousted
They could really tell you
what to paint
Just give them a brush
some red paint
and a blank banner
and you'll find out
in a hurry
what really needs curating
Mama mia

LIBRARY SCENE, MANHATTAN

In the New York Public Library
                    in the men's john
        there's a lot of marble pews
            with a lot of guys in there
                praying that everything
                    will come out all right
One guy looks like Samuel Gompers
                    plotting another strike
Another looks like FDR
        like he's deciding
            to announce a New Deal
Another is maybe the slumming bottom-line editor
                of some publishing conglomerate
                    whom someone sent out to see
                    what a real book looks like
Another is a nobody off the street
        who was snoozing on a park bench
            until he heard Mother Nature call
Along with a ragged clergyman
                who also felt the call
Another looks like a little mafioso
        about to sing
            if he doesn't have to go
                    to Sing Sing
Another looks like the crazy captain
            of this motley crew
        with his funny fisherman's hat askew
                    hiding loose screws

And now of a sudden

                there's a great flushing a great rushing

                    thru clandestine flues

And the whole crew

      in this listing freighter

        laden with all the culture of the world

            sailing on together

                through the postmodern weather

Natural History

Winter's back is broken
The squirrels are out
                    in Central Park
Where
        have they been sleeping?

In the Museum of Natural History
        in its great entrance hall
            a dinosaur rears up
                        protecting its young
    one hundred and forty million
                            years ago
The hall is thronged
            with chattering schoolchildren
        These mammals of all colors
                    pose for pictures
                    under the upraised Barosaurus
He's protecting them too
                from the raptors of the world
No one knows
            what color dinosaurs were
    nor what happened to them
                        or their young
But here they are today
                along with the rest of us
And are we all raptors
        or Advanced Humans

        (as the museum brochures describe us)
          including President Theodore Roosevelt
                    outside the main entrance
             astride a great bronze stallion
                    (oxidizing into green)
And he flanked
        by two brave bronze Indians
                    (also turning green)
And all striding forward together
        into Central Park West
               into the oncoming traffic
                    of the 21st century

SPRING ABOUT TO HAPPEN

Hansom cab through Central Park
                        clop-clop
        white horse pulling
                    the old open carriage
Cabby on the seat
            in his high hat
                        dead asleep
No one in the cab
The horse
        slows to a stop at the curb
The cabby
        keeps sleeping
A couple climbs in
The cabby awakes
                    Where away?
Anywhere!
            cry the two together
                        wrapped in each other
Spring
        is about to happen
A flight of dirty doves
                    takes off from the still-bare trees
The eternal coachman
                    moves his reins
Clop-clop goes the horse
                    Kiss-kiss cry the birds
                            in a song without words

DIRTY TONGUE

The little black dog with the small head and funny tail
enters the little church
during Sunday mass
and waving his tail he wanders up
to where the head priest is praying over microphones
And the dog sniffs the altar
and cocks his head
as if he's listening to the priest
And then he starts sniffing the front-row worshippers
who are now all kneeling
and waiting with eyes closed and open mouths
for Communion
And the priest comes up and starts putting holy wafers
on their extended tongues
and only those with clean tongues
after Confession
are allowed to get the wafer
but the dog raises his paw very politely
and paws the skirt of the priest
with open mouth and tongue hanging out
for he too wants one of those delicious biscuits
But the priest ignores the dog
because the dog has no soul
according to this antique legend
And anyway his tongue is not by any means clean
after all the faces and feces he has licked
And the dog can't get one of these holy biscuits

no such luck for the soulless mutt
who now slinks away
like a starving heathen
on the far far outskirts
of the Roman Empire

BLOOD OF THE BAG LADY

Happy he
    who held those breasts
        apples of bliss
            blissfully hanging
                once upon a time

Now she of the broken bust
stumbles across the street
looking for butts
Old bag of blood
with a history to tell
of where all that blood came from
coursing through generations of generations
all those swimming unsinkable genes
in veins and arteries of the world
sailing through rife humanity
through that beat body
A walking gene pool
teeming tide pool born of oceans
Mother of us all

THE SCREAM HEARD AROUND THE WORLD

One fine day
a proud owner of a brand-new car
started up his infernal combustion engine
and with the first gasp of gas
the whole car gasped
and out of the exhaust pipe emerged
a very small scream
as of a very small animal trapped
in the bowels of the motor
The owner heard it and
thought perhaps a cat or rat
was trapped under the car
He put it in gear
and slowly turned out
into the roadway
But the little scream
didn't stop
He looked back through his mirror
and saw nothing at all
He pulled over and got out and
looked under the machine
There was nothing caught or hanging down
The scream had stopped
when he stopped the car
but when he started up again
the scream arose again
and it grew louder as he

stepped on the gas
He thought he might outrun it
He thought perhaps
if he raced the motor
he could clear it
like a frog in the throat
So he took off down the boulevard
but the faster he went
the louder the scream became
Then he heard all the other cars screaming
and people were hanging out the windows
of all the houses on each side
and holding their ears
looking at all the cars screaming
And as traffic increased at rush hour
a great roar of animal agony
as if all the animals in the world
were caught in all the machines
of the world
And the roaring grew and grew
And the drivers kept on driving
and driving and driving and . . .

First, the News

Sun gets up
shedding light on us
In the wind a linden tree
is whispering
At home in many languages
Intelligence did provide warning
Secretary Steely stated boldly
Military commanders in the field
must have some discretion
Sleeping through the attack
This is Martha Shott in Teheran
Please don't leave me
The Mountains of the Morn
sweep down to the sea
where I met my true love
Overcharges and other frauds
involving a pawnbroker
           a taxi driver
             a pool hustler
               and a tylenol tablet
With managed-care-for-profit
A violin plays between announcements
All Things Considered
and reconsidered
(with a few little exceptions of course)
Don't ever leave me darling
especially at night

We fought Chevron's war
Your heart in a flower
pales the dawn
Rumors of peace
sent the market down
They broke the strike
at Youngstown Sheet & Tube
Thorstein Veblen drank the bitter drink all right
This is Daniel Sure in Washington
A piano plays between bulletins
in an abandoned casino
Pablum for the masses
in the tall grasses
Pol Pot smoked pot
in the jungles of central Cambodia
He wept
It *vill* be interesting
said the terrible Doctor Kissinger
to see the videos
A flower a power a gun
Giving investors a tax break
Oral sex is unspeakably despicable
stated the presiding judge
twisting his tongue
Don't leave me ever
When day is done
The court will modify your conduct
unbecoming an officer
War is good business Invest your son
Oh the eyes of statues the tied tongues of men

looking for a new language
A darkly romantic novel
A hotshot out of West Point
and bodies fall through the skies
Somebody blabbed
We bombed them Ayrabs
back to the Middle Ages
Love me Love my neighbor
History repeats itself
with a stutter
It's all done with mirrors
Managed news Surgical bombing
managed by munition surgeons
Summer Theater presents
Once Upon a Mattress
A fly mates just once and dies
The skies are full of sun & lies
Your heart flowers
after showers
The eyes of statues turn
Loose Lips Sink Ships
and lovers
Don't ever leave me baby
May I have your attention please
Next stop New Orleans Baton Rouge
Next stop Khmer Rouge Lake Charles
Jackson Mississippi
Delta Country Western on the radio
Six men in chain-gang suits
get on a yellow country bus

I had three keys on a ring
three keys of coke
Spent three years in the can
Dexter didn't sing
spent his years in lockdown
A motherly woman in a wig
hands him a copy of Watchtower
Dexter sobs
Dexter breaks down in her arms
The radio sings
Go down Brother Go down
We interrupt this broadcast
They cut off Victor Jara's hands
and he's still singing
They cut off Che Guevara's hands
but he still writes his legend
May I have your attention please
Here I am a sensible man
Am I not Priapus
he of the first spring
In the wind a linden whispering
putting out new leaves of light
reminds me of your heart
Oh Rose of Tralee in the super Mart
I love you

Are There Not Still Fireflies

Are there not still fireflies
Are there not still four-leaf clovers
Is not our land still beautiful
        our fields not full of armed enemies
          our cities never bombed
                by foreign invaders
          never occupied
            by iron armies
                speaking iron tongues
Are not our warriors still valiant
                 ready to defend us
Are not our senators
        still wearing fine togas
Are we not still a great people
        in the greatest country in all the world
Is this not still a free country
Are not our fields still ours
        our gardens still full of flowers
          our ships with full cargoes
Why then do some still fear
        the barbarians coming
          coming coming
             in their huddled masses
   (What is that sound that fills the ear
             drumming drumming?)
Is not Rome still Rome
Is not Los Angeles still Los Angeles

Are these not the last days of the Roman Empire
Is not beauty still beauty
And truth still truth
Are there not still poets
Are there not still lovers
Are there not still mothers
                              sisters and brothers
Is there not still a full moon
                              once a month
Are there not still fireflies
Are there not still stars at night
Can we not still see them
                    in bowl of night
                         signalling to us
                              our manifest destinies?

Into the Interior

astride of a grave, the light gleams for an instant,
then it's night once more

–Samuel Beckett

DON'T CRY FOR ME INDIANA

I feel like I
just got beamed down by Scotty in "Star Trek"
What is this place—Indianapolis 2000?
Out of the sky I got dreamed down
into the Omni Severin Hotel
attached to huge shopping mall all enclosed
all the products of corporate mono-culture
shipped in from somewhere else
"Welcome" says the fancy brochure
"To fabulous fashion, delightful diversions!
Distinct shops entice you to create a new look
Delicate treats tempt you at each and every turn
Opportunities to relax and refresh your spirits abound
With ample parking and enclosed walkways"
All For Sale, including
A 3-foot plaster Venus de Milo only $3229
A $1339 suede jacket
(persuades me not)
A huge windowful of styrofoam breasts
covered by flaming red lace brassieres
(Promise of pneumatic bliss—
Citizens walk by panting)
Where are the fringed buckskin shirts
in the country of Lincoln's boyhood
Where the Indians in Indianapolis
Where the Granger Movement
        the Greenback Party
            the Populist Party

Where Eugene V. Debs when we need him
"Middletown" swept away
All over Middle America the same scene
Mom & Pop neighborhoods boarded up
Don't cry for me Indiana
I've got it made
in the Omni Severin Hotel
Happy men and women in straight suits
walking around with sell phones
National HQ of the American Legion
still just around the corner
But Indian Territory ain't Indian anymore
They've rounded up the Indians and told them
there aren't enough of them
to be called Indians anymore
They fell among the Fallen Timbers
They were tipped over at Tippecanoe
I'm an alien fallen
into this strange land
I came looking for you, Indiana
and what did I find
The settlers are gone, Indiana
And a new breed of pioneers has taken over
Out the seventh floor hotel window
I see the shining cars coming over the horizon
Covered wagons buried long ago
"On the Banks of the Wabash, Far Away"
I hear the cries of the cattlemen in the dusk
The roundup is in full swing
I head out into it

in search of the heart of America
O Hoosier State, who's your state?
A hotel Black man dressed like an admiral
holds the door open for me
Whereaway?

Between Two Cities

Brown stubble cornfields
                by a railroad crossing
                                with sign reading
                                        Uneven Tracks
Bare elms
                like fans against the sky
Furze with birds in a thicket
                                about to fly
A genre farm-painting
                        flashes on my inward eye—
Brown cows by a barn in sun
                                with a dog at play
The lone and level fields
                        stretch away. . . .

THE FREIGHTS

The long freights
   let out their lonely shrieks
      in the Lake Erie dawn
         in fruit of first light
    their boxcars strung out endless
         horizon to horizon
   engines disappeared westward
    and their ends still not visible
       over the cornfields
     the corn itself stacked high
        in the open bins
      cradles rocking
         across America
   toward Huron
      Sandusky
        Port Clinton
          Toledo
Admiral Perry offshore
   sends up his signals
     off Put-In Bay
   The wind shifts
      and his flagship drifts
  Becalmed in the middle distance
    he's raked by British broadsides
    He rows to another ship
      carrying his flag with him
  He closes on the British brigs
    and blasts them with his cannonades
    And carries the day

The battle is won
             for Free Trade
                          and all the Northwest Territory
As Chief Tecumseh shakes his hopeless feather lance
        and disappears over the horizon
And the freights roll on endless
                          over the Northwest Territory
             over the American Empire
                                  past Lake Erie
                                          past Huron
        From Buffalo
             (Gateway to the West—the New Athens!)
        from Cleveland
                 to Detroit
                          to Chicago—(hog-faced brawler!)
Ah but there is an end in sight
Here it comes now
                 as we idle at a crossing
                          red lights flashing
                                  the RR bell ringing
Here comes the end of it
                 the end of all our imaginings
And no caboose
                 no ghost brakeman hanging out
                          from the last platform
                                  railroad cap cocked up
                                          swinging his lantern
Yet still the train cries out
        crying far away like the sea

sending its lonely signal
            to the good townsfolk
                to the good burghers eating burgers
            becalmed in backwaters of
                    shopping malls and filling stations

And Admiral Perry still offshore
                unsure of what bright future
                                    he was fighting for

Appearances of the Angel in Ohio

1.

A loopy angel with one wing
comes out of the P.O.
and gets in a chariot
in the Handicapped Parking zone
and takes off in circles
into the evening sky

2.

Out of town a way
at the deserted Sandusky Drive-In
sitting out in a soybean field
a sign still announcing
'My Best Friend's Wedding'
the loopy angel flies over
dipping her one wing

3.

On Tappan Square in Oberlin Ohio
the temperature is ninety
The fat local dentist waddles out
and falls into the beauty parlor
where his wife is under the dryer
The angel flies in after him
and fans the dried-up ladies

with her wing
as they go on gossipping

4.
A cinematic angel
out of an Italian movie
zooms around the sky
the crane that whirls her
hidden from the cameras
She circles like a rower
with only one oar

5.
Marble orchard with stone angel
as in Thomas Wolfe's Asheville
There she stands tilted
made of white marble
one wing cracked and fallen
into the tall grasses
where lovers kiss asses

6.
It's not every day
one sees one
It takes one to know one
It takes one to be one
You have to be an angel for a day
just to see one

7.
Lake Mohican
and a statue of an Indian
hand to brow
headdress thrown back
The angel with broken wing
flutters down
to smooth his feathers
with her feathered wing
But they do not stay smoothed
They spring up again
bristling at the white angel
this last of the Mohicans

8.
I know this angel is a man
because he has a horn
He flies through the sky
with horn upraised
proclaiming the Last Judgement
even as he fulfills his word
with his flaming sword

9.
Not all angels are true Christians
I met a lay angel once
on the road to Damascus
who was feathering his wing

and flying low and swinging
low over the world
and singing a low song
about sexology
and love and Liberation Theology

10.
One-winged solo flyers
flying toward each other
in the late dusk
like Plato's lost souls
mate and make
one whole angel

11.
A huge moving van with a sign
G.O.D.: Guaranteed Overnight Delivery
lies overturned by the highway
its side sprung open and
a gross of wounded plastic angels spilled out
O you who wept with sorrow here on earth
Don't cry now
that you're back safe in heaven
Broken angels!

Overheard Conversations

Overheard conversations on hot summer nights
by tenement windows
in cities of the world
or in prairie capitals

the lovers on fire escapes
or on front porch swings
plotting their escapes

and the old folk inside
fanning themselves with new newspapers
and rocking

the lovers' words overheard by the old
like lost weekends or trains they never took

the promise of distant kisses
in undiscovered paradises
echoing again
in the hot night's syllables
in the mouths of the young
in the eternal song
still to be re-sung

MOORED

A boat moored
In the deep shade
under a weeping willow
in the bend of a river

As the light fades
so does the boat
with its willow
with its river

Only memory remains
of the lovers
in the bottom of the boat
moored to each other

They too
Gone On

DRINKING FRENCH WINE IN MIDDLE AMERICA

Bought a bottle of Vouvray
and poured out its bouquet
of the French countryside
on the plains of Middle America
and that fragrance
floods over me
wafts me back
to that rainy hillside
by the banks of the Loire
Vouvray tiny village
where I sat with rucksack
twenty-eight years old
seafarer student
uncorking the local bottle
with its captured scent of spring
fresh wet flowers
in first spring rain
falling lightly now
upon me—

Where gone that lonesome hiker
fugace fugitive
blindfold romantic
wanderer traumatic
in some Rimbaud illusionation—

The spring rain falls
upon the hillside flowers

lavande and *coquelicots*
the grey light upon them
in time's pearly gloaming—
Where gone now
and to what homing—
Beardless ghost come back again!

APOLLINAIRE IN AMERICA

Over the high Sierras
flies the plane
And our loves too
Must I remember them again
Joy comes often after pain

Hands upon each other
We lay close together
in halcyon weather
in the high Sierra
long ago

Came the night Tolled the time
From zone to zone the hours pass
And I remain

Love passed slowly long ago
When life was slow
Now time and love are swift
Upon the plane
Time and love go by and I remain

Pass the hours Pass the days
Neither time nor loves
Come back again

Over the far Sierra
flies the plane

INTO THE INTERIOR

I am your whispered voice
your inside voice
your interior voice
your unheard voice
your unspoken voice
your unvoiced voice
your unspeakable voice
I am your heart's voice and your heartless voice
your deepest voice
under layers of living & speaking
the voice of your buried life
your invisible life
your silent life
your unknown life
your unopened life
your unrealized life
the undiscovered life that no one sees
not even your lover
not even yourself

If you will listen to me
if you will lend me the ear
of your mind
and of your bent heart
if you will heed my whisperings . . .
       heed my whisperings . . .
     heed my whisperings . . .
        heed my whisperings. . . .

ALLEN GINSBERG DYING

Allen Ginsberg is dying
It's in all the papers
It's on the evening news
A great poet is dying
But his voice
              won't die
His voice is on the land
In Lower Manhattan
in his own bed
he is dying
There is nothing
to do about it
He is dying the death that everyone dies
He is dying the death of the poet
He has a telephone in his hand
and he calls everyone
from his bed in Lower Manhattan
All around the world
late at night
the telephone is ringing
This is Allen
            the voice says
Allen Ginsberg calling
How many times have they heard it
over the long great years
He doesn't have to say Ginsberg
All around the world

in the world of poets
there is only one Allen
I wanted to tell you he says
He tells them what's happening
what's coming down
on him
Death the dark lover
going down on him
His voice goes by satellite
over the land
over the Sea of Japan
where he once stood naked
trident in hand
like a young Neptune
a young man with black beard
standing on a stone beach
It is high tide and the seabirds cry
The waves break over him now
and the seabirds cry
on the San Francisco waterfront
There is a high wind
There are great whitecaps
lashing the Embarcadero
Allen is on the telephone
His voice is on the waves
I am reading Greek poetry
The sea is in it
Horses weep in it
The horses of Achilles
weep in it

here by the sea
in San Francisco
where the waves weep
They make a sibilant sound
a sibylline sound
Allen
      they whisper
            Allen

ALLEN THIS INSTANT

Allen this instant
was sitting by me
on this bed
just for an instant
or half an instant
there he was
next to me
silent
a fleeting presence
but not fleeting
totally there
between two breaths
Gone as I breathed
sitting next to me
silent and tender
a tender presence
Never sat
on bed with him
never that close
though once he kissed my lips
Now here close as a shadow
his sweet presence
the lush voice silent
not come to speak
to say hello or goodbye
I'd see him again
we'd see each other

once again
for a moment
always fleeting
ephemeral ash
on the wind blown
over some horizon
I haven't known

See you again
dear Allen

ABOUT THE TYPE

This book was set in Garamond, a typeface originally designed by the Parisian typecutter Claude Garamond (1480–1561). This version of Garamond was modeled on a 1592 specimen sheet from the Egenolff-Berner foundry, which was produced from types assumed to have been brought to Frankfurt by the punchcutter Jacques Sabon.

Claude Garamond's distinguished romans and italics first appeared in *Opera Ciceronis* in 1543–44. The Garamond types are clear, open, and elegant.

ABOUT THE AUTHOR

ROBERT D. KAPLAN is a correspondent for *The Atlantic Monthly* and the author of nine previous books on travel and foreign affairs, which have been translated into many languages; these books include *Balkan Ghosts, Eastward to Tartary, Soldiers of God, Warrior Politics,* and *The Ends of the Earth.* He lives in western Massachusetts.

ALLEN STILL

Allen died 49 nights ago, and in Bixby Canyon now the white
misshapen moon sailed listing through the sky all night across
the horizon above this bowl of hills followed by a white star,
no fog in the morning, bright and clear, warm air for this
hour, birds up early telling their night's stories always differ-
ent always the same, so few notes to tell the tale, just before
first light, moon fading on western rim of canyon, the follow-
ing star washed out by sun's first lighting, willows and yellow
lupin and yellow mustard blossoms and cactus and bell-
shaped white morning glory reaching up silent exulting (We
are alive and breathing!) the woods full of tiny life teeming,
tiny lives chirring in the dense green, under the lush willows,
beeches and dying alders. . . . Lorenzo and lady still asleep,
she two months pregnant (conceived perhaps the night Allen
died) . . . he pregnant in the earth now though cremated
and buddhist spirit exited through top of head, his burnt dust
now feeding some other embryo bird or frog. . . . What will
arise from it, from him, dusty *passageur*?

BLIND POET   (*To be performed with a blindfold*)

I am your blind poet and painter
I am contemplating my navel
I see my own insides
I see my own mind
full of fantastic phrases and images
I am painting the landscape of my soul
and the soul of mankind
as I see it
I am giving it a voice
I am singing folk songs
about the workers
I am singing about the downtrodden masses
and the rich on their fat asses
I am the painter who feels
with his fingers
I am the blind seeing-eye poet
I see what you can't see
I eat well and drink well
and dream of great epics
I am your postmodern pastmodern multi-media artist
I am the most avant of the avant
I'm site-specific and totally conceptual
Even the greatest critics have been baffled
by my profundity
I once knew Andy Warhol
I've slept with you know whom
And I'm a fast-speaking man

I am your deconstructed language poet
your far-out poet
full of ecstasies and visions
your wandering workshop poet
your university poet
with tenure
your buddhist quietest poet
I go on poetry reading tours
where everything is paid for
I hear everything
and it's grist to my mill
I use it all
to make great sound poetry
or great concrete poetry
that no one can see through
Life is a real dream
and I am dreaming it
And I've got it all in my head
the Song of Humanity
and the Song of Inhumanity
I'll paint you a profound picture
an action painting
a gestural painting
nothing but pure gesture
I'll write you a far-out song
of common people
If I take off my mask
I'll see the real world
for the first time
But I won't take it off

It fits too well
It's a perfect fit
It's too comfortable
And I've got my career to think of
my life to think of
We only live once
and living well is the best revenge
Get your own blindfold
You can't have mine
You'll have to face the world without it
And anyway I'm too young to die
I'm an American
and Americans don't die
We're the conquerors
We're the new roman emperors
We're conquering the world
with global capitalism
I can see it but you can't see it
It's the Invisible Empire
And democracy *is* capitalism
No more poor people
No more Huddled Masses
in our empire
The rising tide lifts all boats!
No more people starving and dying
No more hunger and torture and death
So get smart, get with it
Hang my painting!
Publish my poem!

MOUTH

I'm tired of my mouth
It's too small
and it doesn't say enough
doesn't sing enough
and it doesn't emit light
like your eyes
It's always clamming up
when it should be singing
or sounding off
It's thin-lipped and stubborn
It's essentially a closed mouth
I've been trying to open it wider
all my life
There's just some things it can't say
though the heart prompts it
It's a mouth with an overbite
although it never bites anyone alive
Just dead animals
and it used to eat
everything in sight
It's had various battles
with dead cows pigs lambs rabbits buffalo
and birds of various feather
and always succeeded in chewing them up
He's a real asshole this mouth
a proto-fascist playing censor
always suppressing some thought

instead of liberating it
This mouth of mine
always opening and closing
at the wrong time
speaking out
when he should be holding his tongue
his sharp little tongue
added to the fact that I
am always putting a foot in it
This mouth of mine
has been through a great deal
But it never learns
It just keeps saying
the dumbest things
the stupidest things
in several languages
which it always acts as if it knows fluently
What a *farceur*
what a mimic
what a copycat
what an outright fraud
It's not a bad mouth
though he's bad-mouthed some people
It's not a loud-mouth anyway
It's just trying to be a good mouth
to perform its essential function
And why not?
It has to eat to live
But does it have to talk also?
Perhaps I'll join the Trappists

All I know is
I'm fed up with this mouth
This mouth that's been feeding me
all these years
that's been kissing people for me
and trying to do a lot of other things to people
on my behalf
Anyway I'm stuck with it
There's no changing it
I can't sew it up
So what am I to do with it
except keep accepting
what it eats for me
what it says for me
And who knows
maybe someday
it'll break right open
and blurt right out
some great poetry
in some primal tongue
made of love and light and dung
some great immortal song
no human ever heard before
nor ever sung

A TOURIST OF REVOLUTIONS

And I was a tourist of revolutions
a dilettante of revolutions
I was Whitey
without a revolution of my own
(or so I thought)
People are starving & dying
So I had to join Third World revolutions
I was a Fidelista in 1959
I was a Sandinista in 1989
I thought I was one of them
(and perhaps I was)
They called me *campañero*
They published my poems
in their revolutionary papers
In "Lunes de Revolución"
they called me *poeta*
(which means a lot down there)
On Monday of the Revolution
I was a gringo poet
right in line with their line
People are starving & dying
The other days of the week
back home or wherever
I might have been something else
Who knows what
a poetic hustler a poor man's painter
A smalltime businessman

son of a smalltime mafioso
In *Havana libre*
I shook Fidel's friendly hand
in a people's cafeteria
I went to Hemingway's bar
and looked around
but didn't say anything
and never asked why Papa Hem
hemmed and hawed
and never spoke out for Fidel
(He went fishing instead)
I never turned my head
I was a tourist and a good one
Here today Gone tomorrow
People are starving & dying
And when I die without a sound
   And when I die without a sound
I'll surely join I'll surely join
                the permanent Underground

And Lo

And lo a star arose in the east
only it was the sun
and three wise guys or goys
spied it and exclaimed
Behold, Great God Sun
creator of light
creator of all life on earth
without which we would live in darkness
forever and ever
Great God Sun
bringer of the only light we know
and the only god we have visual proof really exists
the only god
who's not an invention of our desperate imaginations
seeking some way out or up
beyond certain death
Great God Sun
creator of night and day on earth
there are no gods before you
And lo
a babe was born in a manger
by immaculate conception or spontaneous combustion
and there was great rejoicing
out there in the desert
and the babe arose and spake
in a loud voice
Yeah man it's a fact

I am born of God the Father great god Sun
and I am his Holy Ghost on earth
which he in his heavenly wisdom
sent to you in the form of light
and I am that light
which is love on earth forever and ever
Amen!

INDEX